The Time Is Now;

Awaken Your Dormant Gifts

By

Edie Darling

Isabelle —

May the spirit of the living God fall fresh upon you as you read this book — Go to higher heights

Peace + Blessings

Edie Darling

8/27/19

The Time Is Now; Awaken Your Dormant Gifts
By Edie Darling

© 2019 Edie Darling
Printed in the United States of America

ISBN 978-1-7329400-8-6

All Biblical quotes, unless otherwise noted, are from the New International Version.

Published by: The Ghost Publishing
Author: Edie Darling
Edited by: Eli Gonzalez
Proofread by: Christine James
Contact info: <u>Awakenyourdormantgifts@gmail.com</u>
Cover Design: The Ghost Publishing

Testimonials

Compelling. Edie Darling vividly demonstrates with boldness and clarity on the prophetic like no other as she helps re-introduce you to Abba Father. *That* God, the God of the impossible. Amazingly, there is no fear of being politically correct here. I almost fell off my chair when I read, "man found a way to bastardize it (God's word) for their own gains." She's talking about the Word of Truth. Such a controversial topic is surely suggested in today's circles, just not discussed so openly. The breadth and scope of this book will stimulate your thinking as you explore this modern day revelation of the God of Abraham, Isaac & Jacob.

Naomi Powell

Executive Pastor

Director Missions/Outreach

Countryside Christian Church/Clearwater, FL

Edie Darling is a fierce advocate for the Word of God, through her work as a Life Coach, Mentor, Inspirational Leader and Author. Edie challenges readers to cast out fear while eloquently and joyously igniting a passion for living an intentional, God-centered life, utilizing our God-given gifts to fulfill our purpose on this earth. Her steadfast conviction, inspiring message and exuberant delivery will entice any reader to go faithfully farther than ever before and never look back.

Be prepared for truly divine inspiration.

Bridget Joiner-Figgener

Investigative Analyst

Federal Bureau of Investigation

The Time is now; Awaken Your Gifts, is a must read whether you're in ministry, feel called to ministry, or just came to know the Lord. Edie's written voice is clear and authoritative. This book will speak to you in a manner that few, if any, ever have.

Eli Gonzalez

CEO and Editor

The Ghost Publishing

I've had the privilege of publishing more than a thousand Christian books. *This* book is special. It grabbed my full attention from beginning to end. Rarely do you see such a bold book written with such compassion and clarity.

Peter Lopez

Senior Publisher

Xulon Press

This is a powerful read!

"My eyes were amazed at the feat my hand was doing as it wrote out God's message in a way I had never been taught."

Be prepared to see *That* God, the God of miracles, do something only He can do. It is profoundly thought-provoking. The level of discernment given to her by God himself will uplift and edify any reader, regardless of their background.

Bishop Herson

Vida Church

Rhode Island and Massachusetts

Foreword

I met Edie Darling in 2014 when she came to the Library of Congress to get assistance in determining what language she could write, read, and translate. This unique divine ability came to me as a surprise and to others as well. I'm not a linguist, but I am an African Area Specialist and it was amazing for me to see her symbolic writings.

I thought it would be an easy task to assist Edie in identifying the language. We know the language she writes is an extinct ancient language, which confounds the minds of many leading experts. What makes finding the answer all the more challenging is because you have to be willing to dig deep archaeologically. It has been nearly five years of diligent research; however I believe we are on the brink of finding truth stemming from biblical times.

Researchers are unearthing ancient writings going back to the 25th Dynasty of Egypt hidden in the depths of the pyramids. One expert said: *Edie's writings look like one of the Canaanite Languages.* Because of a recent congressional inquiry to know the original languages of Africa before outside influences, Edie was encouraged to seek her congressman's assistance in her search for answers.

There was a time when God was angry with His people, confused their language and scattered them abroad at the Tower of Babel. They weren't listening to God and He separated them from the One True Language. The more research I am able to do, I believe she carries the One True Language of the I AM THAT I AM, the God of our forefathers, the God of Abraham, the God of Isaac and the God of Jacob.

I personally believe *The Time Is Now* for Edie Darling to share the messages God has given her with the world. Due to the current climate we are living in, her message could not be more relevant for God's people today.

Marieta Harper, Area Specialist

African & Middle Eastern Division - **Library of Congress**

Dedication

This book is dedicated to the God of our forefathers...

The God of Abraham

The God of Isaac

and

The God of Jacob (Israel)

Table of Contents

Chapter 1

Time and Tide Waits on No Man

Time

My mother used to tell me, "Time and tide waits on no man." Meaning, both ways of measuring the passing of time, either the man-made version of the years, months, weeks, days, hours, and seconds of a clicking clock – or the God made version of measuring the passing of time by the tides that coincides with the change of season and the gravitational pull in relation to the moon, sun, and stars – they keep going whether you like it or not.

Time happens all the time. The problem for many is that they spend too much of their time focusing on their past while others spend too much of it spent focusing on their future. The most important period of time God ever gave you is this time right now – the present.

I submit to you that while you read this, this very moment in time has been ordained from since the beginning of time. God has given me a message for you and it's getting to you right when it had to. This message is not late and this message is not early. If you're reading this book, regardless of your present circumstances, this message is getting to you right on time.

Here the message: *The Time is Now.*

Just for the record, yes, I'm talking to you.

How much longer will you live an unfulfilled life? How much longer will you stay in this slump? I know you're tired of the same old, same old. You don't like your job, you don't like your co-workers, and you sure don't like your pay. You may not even like some family members right now. You're sick and tired of being sick and tired and you've become a *walking dead*, a person who goes about an unfulfilling routine.

You're exhausted, yet because you've confused movement and activity with progress, you haven't gotten anywhere. You need to sit down and take a good deep breath. A long time ago, a man took his first breath. The

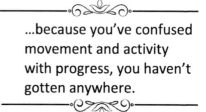

...because you've confused movement and activity with progress, you haven't gotten anywhere.

name given to him was Adam. God breathed life into him, transforming him from a sculpture of dirt and mud into the person who was given dominion over every living creature on the planet.

It's time to shake off the old clothes, the old labels, the old way of thinking you wouldn't amount to much. Those old views say that everyone is out to get you because you're a person of color, or a woman, or because you live below the poverty line or because you're too old or too young – or too skinny or too fat or too lazy or too sickly or too black or too white or not educated enough or not pretty enough or not tall enough, or you don't have the right connections or the right pedigree, or anything else the father of lies has used to allow you to believe that you aren't going to do great things in your life.

Let me remind you that each of God's chosen have been given a territory to affect for His Kingdom. God has given you people, places, organizations, and communities to influence. You have been called to do something special, something life-changing to many. That's not a trivial matter.

God has equipped you with gifts and talents suitable for a time such as this. My question is – what have you done with them? Why do they lie dormant?

God says, "Even before I could finish my sentence, you ask of Me: *how*? The question *how*, should not be asked at this time. In time I will send those people your way who will help you understand what it is I want you to do. Do not be afraid, do not allow your mind to worry. Continue to pray, continue to seek Me first. It may seem as though things are changing fast for you, but stand steadfast in My name.

"Fear is only what you allow it to be. I am not to be afraid of. You are my child and I will not forsake you.

"When you take dominion over what I have given, you will realize how powerful you are and the following of people you have influence over. "

Reintroduction to the Father

We have become so Jesus-centric, many of us believers have forgotten about the Father. We know Jesus was and is the son of God. We know when He left, the Holy Spirit – the Comforter – was sent to us as a lineage of Jesus. But somewhere along the way, many have forgotten the Father. We have forgotten the beginning.

In this book, I'm going to re-acquaint many of you to Abba Father. You may have heard the term, *Abba* mentioned before but never understood it. It's actually a way to reference a father by a term of intimate endearment. Simply translated, it's the defining term for, father, in the Aramaic language, spoken by Jesus and Paul as an intimate term to characterize their personal relationships with God.

In fact, Paul only used it twice in the Bible whereas Jesus only used it once. He was hanging on a cross, on the verge of mortal death, when he said, captured in Mark 14:36, "Abba Father, all things are possible for you. Take this cup from Me; nevertheless, not what I will, but what You will." That verse, to me, is the most intimate words Jesus ever spoke. It speaks of a relationship with the Father no one who had lived had ever experienced. That's the type of relationship God, the Father, wants with you.

I decree and declare that as you read this, you're about to be set free. Mind-traps of the enemy are about to be

There will be an awakening of your spirit...

made clear and fall off. There will be an awakening of your spirit and much of the old man that you struggle with will pass away and your future will be made anew.

I grew up in St. Petersburg, Florida. My family didn't have much in terms of money. You could say I was just another black female growing up with the regular challenges we face. But then, God did something miraculous through me. He stirred up my spirit in a manner like never before.

The feeling was so new and rare, I have a difficult time describing it, but it was as if God downloaded messages on my mind and spirit that I couldn't keep to myself. I had to let it out. I sat down to write what God was telling me and something supernatural occurred – I started writing... but it wasn't in English!

My eyes were amazed at the feat my hand was doing as it wrote out God's message in a way I had never been taught. Some people have described the writings as hieroglyphics. I stared at what God had written through me, amazed at His power. I showed it to a few people but they had no idea what I had put on paper. It seemed like a language long dead.

In 2010, my search for its origins brought me to Egypt, where a Shaman man recognized it as an ancient language. At the behest of many people, I then brought it to the

Library of Congress in 2014. I was a little apprehensive as to how these writings would be perceived – the writings of a black woman from St. Petersburg who said God had downloaded writings from her in a language that is perhaps long dead – the wrong person could have forever snuffed out all hope that they would take a serious look at it.

I'm so thankful it was Ms. Marieta Harper who God placed there to see my writings. For one, I'm thankful she didn't think I was crazy! For two, because of her, my writings sit at the Library of Congress as of the time of this writing, where they have been recognized as an extinct ancient language. You can get a thousand times *No,* but one *Yes* can change the trajectory of your life.

But, the fact that little ole' me wrote it is only half the miracle. The other half is that I could interpret it!

In this book, I will share with you many of the letters God had *downloaded* on me. You will see a rare glimpse of the Father and the Son as they pass on a timely and life-changing exhortation to their people.

In preparing you for the words of God, there are things you must read for your spirit to be receptive to His message. Know this, you were set free the moment you accepted Jesus. Now, it's time to walk out your destiny to its fulfillment.

NOTES

What did God reveal to you in this chapter?

Chapter 2

How it all Began

How did this happen? Where did it all begin?

Some people God chooses. Some people chase after God. I found myself in both positions when I pursued God after the death of my sister Lila in 1995. I pursued God like chasing after a criminal. Why do I say a criminal? You have to remember I was in law enforcement, so the one thing I knew was the intensity that goes behind bringing someone to justice. That's the intensity I had when I went into hot pursuit of God. That pursuit of God continued for three years. At the time, I thought I was going into pursuit of God, but in actuality God was in hot pursuit of me.

On October 18, 1998, my church was scheduled to visit a sister church in Sanford, Florida. It seemed that, prior to my family and me visiting the church, the devil was trying to keep us from going. Our family had rented a minivan and I was the only one available to drive us there.

My daughter, who suffered from asthma, was having a terrible time and had to be taken to the hospital twice. She was taken to the hospital the night before our visit to the church and then again, on the morning of. On both trips to the hospital, she was released and given medication. I felt the devil was working overtime trying to keep us from going. My family and I were all thinking, "Maybe we shouldn't go, seeing that Candice is not feeling well."

But I kept praying. I knew if I could only go to church in Sanford, I would receive a blessing. I felt it in my spirit! I didn't realize the magnitude of blessing I would be receiving, but I was going expecting a blessing. I wasn't going to allow the devil to keep me from receiving something that was rightfully mine. I just kept praying and believing God, and I knew His will would be done.

> I wasn't going to allow the devil to keep me from receiving something that was rightfully mine.

Eventually, my daughter felt well enough for us to take the trip. We all loaded up in the minivan and headed for Sanford with my daughter's medication in hand. We played gospel music the entire way there. I was so excited, and I wanted to praise God, thanking Him for allowing us to make the trip.

My mom made arrangements for my uncle and his daughter, who live in Sanford, to meet us at the church. It seemed like a family reunion, but we were there for the sole purpose of praising God.

The service began and, as the choir marched into the sanctuary singing praises to our Lord, it was only a matter of moments before I began jumping up and down and shouting. As some would say, "I got the Holy Ghost."

Again, I couldn't keep still – it was like fire shut up in my bones. I eventually settled down, but as our pastor preached the Word of God, I heard him say, "And Jesus rose on the third day!" I felt the fire raging in my spirit. I couldn't keep still. I was sitting next to my cousin, who suddenly held onto me. It was at that moment when I began to speak in an unknown language.

I heard someone from the crowd say, "She's speaking African." My eyes were closed; I was under the true anointing of God. I had experienced a true encounter with God and what a wonderful feeling it was.

I was removed from the sanctuary and taken into the lobby area of the church. The Spirit of God was upon me so strong, then He began to give me a vision. God showed me I needed to speak with a man in church who was dressed in a striped suit and tie – his life depended on it. God showed me he was sitting in the rear of the church.

Members of my church came out to check on me to see if I was okay. I told them about the man I needed to see. They went inside the church to try to locate him, but to no avail.

It seemed like hours later, but as I was about to go back inside, a man exited out of the sanctuary dressed exactly the way God had showed me.

I approached him and asked him if I could touch him, and at that time, God gave him a Word. Out of concern, my mother said to me, "You can't go asking people if you can touch them!" I knew I had to ignore my mother and obey God.

After I made contact with him, other people came up to me and they, too, were given a Word from God. Many times I was told, "There's no way you could have known that but it be given you from God. I've never shared that with anyone but God."

My mother worried. She didn't understand what was happening. She grew up in tradition and this went outside the scope of her traditions. She later told me she felt I'd had a nervous breakdown because I had taken my sister's death hard.

Because the Anointing of God was so heavily upon me, my mother was frantically trying to find someone to drive the minivan home for us. I reassured her I was okay to drive us home and I did. I explained, "I'm just filled with the Holy Spirit."

Wow … I went to church expecting a blessing, but who could have ever imagined the magnitude of His Blessings?

As I look back upon my childhood, I can remember hearing, "Tongues aren't real, they're of the devil and people who speak it are just babbling." But here it was, I was speaking in an unknown tongue. I had what I like to call a *Day of Pentecost* experience.

God's Hands were moving mightily on me that night!

After I dropped everyone off safely, I arrived home and I couldn't sleep. I was up to the wee hours of the morning. The Holy Spirit told me to write. As I began to write, it wasn't in English. It was in an unknown language, a language (Scripts) that I had never seen or written before.

NOTES

What did God reveal to you in this chapter?

Chapter 3

I AM THAT I AM

The Sword of the Spirit

Over time, man found a way to take God's Scripture, His Word, the lamp that guides our feet, the Book of the Law, the Gospel, the Living Word, the Sword of the Spirit, the Word of Life, and found a way to bastardize it for their own gains. The Word of Truth became used to provide credibility for man's personal goals and fixations. Since the foundation of this earth God had a plan for his written Word, but many have traded the message of hope and eternal salvation for earthly riches that span a mere sixty or eighty years.

I can only guess how it started, but I'm imagining that someone got upset at someone else who had a difference of opinion and, not knowing how else to win the argument, said that God agreed with him. He then went to take verses out of context to prove his point. That's been happening even since before the days of Jesus. When Jesus argued with the Pharisees – the very people who upheld the Holy Scriptures – who thought He was going against God's writings. Do you get the irony of that? "Holy" men not seeing the Messiah for who he is, instead thinking He's trying to destroy their faith!

Jesus answered, and I'm paraphrasing (you can read the actual content in Matthew 5: 17), "I came to fulfill the law, not destroy it! But you've put additional stipulations and restrictions on God's chosen people making it harder for them to know who God is!"

In essence, I think part of what Jesus was saying was, "You've changed it! No, no, no, this ain't gonna work. Somewhere along the way, the message has been changed. We got to take this back to the beginning."

The Blueprint

When builders build a house or building, they follow a blueprint. Meaning, someone – in this case, an architect who understands the laws of physics – determines how much each material weighs, the durability of items, how much space is required in each room to facilitate its purpose, and much more. They had to expertly analyze the reason for the edifice and create a master plan on how to build it so that it fulfills its purpose.

In the same way, God has given each of us a blueprint to follow.

God gave each of us a vision, for you it may have been in the days of your youth, but few have said, "Send me, Lord. I'll go." And now that time has continued on, we have forgotten that calling, which seemed like a lifetime ago. God is telling us to go back to the foundation.

Interestingly enough, my Bible is actually blue. So, when I say, *the Bible is the blueprint*, I literally mean my Bible is my blue print! And when I think of going back to the foundation – I think of Genesis 1, when it states that the Spirit of the Lord hovered above the waters... see, when God first created the heavens and earth, for a while there was only water. Water is blue. The foundation, the Word of God, is the Blue Print you need to follow. If you can go back to the beginning with God, like His Spirit hovered over the water, so shall it hover over and through you.

...we have forgotten that calling, which seemed like a lifetime ago.

THAT GOD

We all know *about* God. But do you know, *that* God?

Rahab did. She was the Canaanite prostitute that lived in the city of Jericho. When the Israelite spies came into the city and needed to escape, she saw *that God* in them. She said, again, I'm paraphrasing, "I've never met you guys before, but I heard of your God. He's that God that has done powerful things. If He said He's about to level the city, I know He will. Come inside, I'll help you."

Jericho was demolished and the only ones who were spared were Rahab and her family. Because she recognized the spirit of God that hovered over the Israelites, she became a lineage to Jesus.

Do you know, *that God*? When was the last time your spirit was touched by that God and not just during praise and worship? When was the last time you were convicted by that God and really desired real change, or as Jesus said it, "go, and sin no more?"

Do you pray to a God that is your buddy, someone you mutter what you'd like to happen under your breath while stopped at a red light? You know what I'm talking about. You're at a red light, about to go to a meeting and you mutter, "Oh Lord, let this meeting go well." And then you continue on. Are your prayers more like wishful thinking or hopeful suggestions? That's not how our God wants to communicate with you.

That God is not the God of Abraham, Isaac, and Jacob. *That* God is not the God that parted the red seas or that brought down fire from above. When Moses asked God, "Who should I say sent me?" God answered, "Tell them I'm the God of your forefathers." They knew *that God.* *That* God had done astonishing, miraculous things! I want to re-introduce you to *that God,* the God of the impossible. The God of miracles. The God who commanded while in the darkness, "Let there be light!" And saw that the light was good.

That same God put light inside of you. And He sees you as good. *That* God delights in you and has plans for you. Your light shines bright, but man has tried to dim that light. But you're reading this because God wants you to know He's about to illuminate you and bring you to the next level. You're getting ready to walk into a year of great explosion.

Yes, You!

One of the biggest lies of the enemy is to make us think, because we're not perfect, God won't use us. Let me share a secret with you... God will use anyone. Probably the two biggest figures in the Old Testament weren't saints. Moses was a murderer and David was worse, he was an adulterer and a murderer. You see yourself as unworthy because you have not forgiven

Wake up! God has already forgiven you.

yourself for what you've done. Wake up! God has already forgiven you. You are set free! The jail doors have been blasted open. All you have to do is walk to your freedom.

You've walked the path to freedom before but you may have lost your way, so I'll remind you of it. Jesus sacrificed himself on the cross, when you got baptized you made a covenant to accept Him as your personal Lord and Savior, then He washed away all sin and all things became new. You're about to enter into a new season where all things are going to be made new again. This present moment is the beginning of your new season. Walk out of your self-imposed bondage and walk into your calling.

Stop seeing yourself as a failure, as someone who can't do anything right, as someone who is in a failed marriage, a failed job, has failed as a parent because your kids don't serve the Lord. Stop listening to dream killers and dream stealers. They may say they love you but, follow me here, they don't even comprehend that they want what you have but aren't qualified to

> Stop listening to dream killers and dream stealers.

carry out your calling – so they tell you that you are less than what you are. Regardless of where you are in your life, God can still use you to do great things. The matter now is that you have to see yourself as God sees you. You, who are made in his perfect image. *That God* has equipped you for the destiny He has ordained you.

When you step into your purpose, when you step onto your stage, you don't have to worry about who is going to be there and who's not, you have nothing to prove to anybody. You do your part, God will do His. You just walk in faith, talk in faith, plan in faith, and manifest what's in your power to manifest in faith, and God will do the rest.

I AM THAT I AM

God told me, "Edie, I want you to forget everything you think you know about Me and allow Me to reveal Truth to you."

I told my mother, you can tell mamma anything – she answered, "I don't know about that, Edie…"

But the Creator revealed to me His truth. The type of truth that sets captives free. God told me, "Go back to the beginning and find Me."

I knew within myself there was more than what was being preached from the pulpit. More than *He died and rose again*. Every time I went to church, I was told I was going to hell. If I wore my hair a certain way, if I wore makeup, everything I did seemed to be sending me to hell. I was like, "How do I get out of hell?" Jesus said he came to set the captives free. That scripture manifested itself into reality in my life and I was set free, indeed.

One of the truths I realized is, it's hard to forget what man told you about God. Everything we think about God has been ingrained in us for so long we have forgotten what's real and what's not, what's important to know and what's not.

Abraham was a friend of God's. God wants that same friendship with you. His Son already atoned for your sins by the shedding of His blood. Shake the shackle of guilt away already. Forget about the divisions in your church community. Just seek Him. Forget about all the denominations. Just seek Him. Forget about what color you are. Just seek Him. Stop worrying about your finances, your romantic relationships, and your constant

> Shake the shackle of guilt away already.

need for entertainment and just seek Him. If you seek Him you will find Him. Allow Him to reveal His truth in you.

Seek the God of your spiritual forefathers. When you identify with *that God,* he will identify himself through you and in you and you'll be able to take back what has been stolen from you. You will inherit what He has given you since you were in your mother's womb.

I declare, God's about to make your crooked path straight. Don't look to the left. Don't look to the right. You have been handed the blueprint. Construct your success in Him. In the end, nothing else matters.

NOTES

What did God reveal to you in this chapter?

Chapter 4

The Walking Dead

Far too many of God's people have been lulled into a spiritual slumber. We, who have once heard the voice of the Shepherd, have allowed extraneous circumstances to mold us and categorize us. They have allowed the world to define who they are, and as a result, their identities have been compromised.

They have taken on the identity of those around them, their culture, their tax bracket, their native language – and they don't know how powerful they are in the hands of the living God. They have taken on the identities of their mothers, fathers, jobs, surroundings, etc., and don't realize the true cloak of identity given to them since the beginning of time. They are... the walking dead.

Let me tell you this, *if you allow the world to define you, it will confine you.*

Spiritually, they struggle to grow. Instead of giving off fruits of the Spirit, they project vast wastelands of wasted potential in Christ Jesus. Much like the Israelites once they were freed from Egypt, they wander around aimlessly for years without getting to where God told them to get to.

Out of all of God's chosen people who were freed from bondage, only Joshua and Caleb entered into the Promised Land. They traveled a long, arduous forty years to travel an eleven-day journey! I'm here to tell somebody reading this book that you don't have to wait a lifetime to walk out your calling! Just don't be like the generation of Israelites who never fully realized what God had done for them.

God had freed them from perhaps the most powerful nation in their time. In the long view of the history of mankind, Egypt was one of the mightiest nations to ever rule. That's whom God freed them from. Similarly, God has freed you from the slavery of sin and death – mighty foes. God made it so the Pharaoh could never chase after them again, much like God did with you with the people He has taken out of your life.

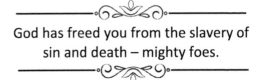

God has freed you from the slavery of sin and death – mighty foes.

Yet, the people still complained!

These are the same people that saw the plagues, such as the massive invasion of locusts. They heard the cries of the Egyptian parents early in the morning hours as they realized their firstborns were dead, while their offspring was kept safe. They walked over dried ground from what was previously the bottom of an ocean floor. And in the wilderness, where there was not enough food to sustain them all, they ate the God-given Manna. They saw the cloud that led them during the day and the pillar of fire that led them at night. Yet, they still complained!

I'll tell you why. Although they were divinely and miraculously delivered out of physical captivity, they remained enslaved mentally. They couldn't identify as free people, even though they had escaped bondage and crossed into borders of freedom. Instead of worshipping and thanking Yahweh, they murmured and complained.

In the same way, if we look back at all God has done for us, we, who have been set free, have much to be thankful for. God has not only extended His Grace and Mercy to us, but also to our children who act as if they never knew God, sometimes because of us. We forget how hard we prayed for a good job, a good spouse, and a good place to live and we complain about having to wake up early for the job that supports our families, we complain about our spouses who do mostly everything right, and we complain about our homes, as we sit down to eat a hot meal in comfort and safety. And just like the generations of Israelites that died in the wilderness, many of God's children are dying in the wilderness and will never reach the land of milk and honey.

Have you been blinded by your circumstances? Do you identify as your gender, race, nationality, hood, or income level? Or do you first identify yourself as a servant of the Living God? Have you forgotten to give thanks to God for all He has already done in your life or are you complaining about lacking creature comforts, because you continue to compare yourself to others? Have you allowed your past hurts, torments, and pains to map out your future? What is it that has kept you back from walking out the fullness of God's purpose in your life?

Nothing God did for the Israelites seemed to be good enough. Sound familiar?

I decree and declare a holy liberation will come over your mind, body, and spirit as you continue to read this book. Tell the enemy – *the Devil is a lie* (excuse my Ebonics) and that your time complaining is over as you enter into a season of praising.

Spiritual Suicide

I once had a conversation with a dear friend that rocked me to my core. He was complaining about his life, like many people do, and perhaps he was expecting me to have sympathy for him, as many do when they hear someone complain. He hadn't realized that I'm not one to accept people's excuses, I'm too busy pointing out to others what God wants to do in each of our lives.

So, after he finished, I asked him, "Are you ready for change?" I thought it was an easy question. He was obviously not happy where he was in life, so I figured he'd be excited for a change.

Here's when he rocked me. He answered, "I don't think so. I think it's too difficult to change and it would be easier for me to stay the same."

Spiritual suicide!

He literally chose to become a member of the walking dead. My friend now is 'Stuck like Chuck.' The worst part is, he wasn't forced or coerced into it. He knows the truth that sets people free, he just refuses to walk in truth.

People like him may not intend to, but they speak death everywhere they go. Matthew 12:34 says, and I'm paraphrasing – *the mouth speaks out of the abundance of the heart.* Being that their hearts are not filled with the power of resurrection and of love, peace, and joy, they are naysayers,

"That will never work."

"I can't do that."

"They'll never listen to me."

"Don't branch out on your own."

"God couldn't have called you for that."

Their tongues have become their anthem of destruction. As they sow seeds of wastelands for others, they condemn their own lives.

Gang-Bangers

People aren't born wanting to profit off of other people's miseries. Yet, at times, our surroundings engulf us to becoming a product of where we come from. I believe that's why people join gangs. It's not that they have more evil than others, it's *more* because that's all they know. Your perspective on life determines the actions you take.

Saul, who later became known as Paul, went on to write much of the New Testament. He was also a product of his environment. He was born into a culture where the – eye for an eye – law had to be protected jealously, or, as he demonstrated, by any means necessary. So he made it his business to hunt down the people who would challenge the law by acknowledging a man named Jesus as the Messiah. But on the road to Damascus, while on a mission for the enemy, his perspective changed.

I'm told I was quite an angry child at times. Things got worse for me when my father passed away when I was eighteen years old. I was contentious, fighting with everybody. My auntie told me, "Edie, you are so powerful. Contained in you is the ability to destroy the world. I'd like for you to change the negative into a positive though, and not destroy the world, but to save it." I went on to have an intimate and personal encounter with Jesus and now, many years later, I'm impacting the Kingdom of God instead of using my gifts and abilities for evil.

Saul was angry too. I would dare say he felt justified when he killed Christians. The anger was like a haze over his eyes and he couldn't see that he was on a path of destruction, not liberation. Like me, and most likely like you, Saul heard the voice of the Lord. What is interesting to me is that it was the first time he heard that voice, yet instantly he knew the voice of the shepherd. "Is that you, Lord?" He asked. Saul died on the road to Damascus. Paul became an agent of change. He went on to use every ounce of his gifts to further the Kingdom of God on earth.

It's Time to Wake up

It's time to let go of whatever anger fuels you to drive you away from your calling. It has shifted your view of the world and your place in it. It has buried your gifts, your smiles, and your voice.

There is a deeper meaning for your existence. Read on and hear directly from God, what He wants to say to you.

NOTES

What did God reveal to you in this chapter?

Chapter 5

Find Your Voice

I told my mother, "I know what I want to be when I grow up."

My mother leaned into me with a warm smile. I was fourteen or fifteen at the time. She had a feeling she knew what I was going to say.

"A police officer," I answered.

My mother stood up straight, taken aback by my answer. She put her right hand on my left shoulder and leaned into me again. "No, sweetie," she said. "You want to be a nurse."

"No Mommy, I want to be a police officer."

An hour before this conversation, my two older brothers had run inside the house from fixing the car. They were cussing. You didn't come to momma's house cussing so something must have really gone wrong.

"We were robbed at gunpoint!"

Mom said, "We need to call the police."

I yelled *NO* – it had been ingrained in me that police officers were not to be trusted. We weren't the type of people to call the police.

A white officer came in and treated our family with the utmost respect. Mom even let him sit at our dinner table. Before he left, he shook each of our hands. When he shook mine, I felt a transference of power. I've now been a Police Officer for more than two decades.

It's easy to want to be what people who love you want you to be, instead of who God destined you to be. For the most part, they don't try to manipulate you, they believe they see your strengths and weaknesses and try to help you use them in a way that would make life easier for you. As good as their intentions might be, you'll almost never find your true voice that way.

There are millions of believers whose voices have been silenced. Maybe you were married with someone who said he/she would support you, but you found yourself putting in most of your time and energy supporting his/her dreams. Maybe you thought you knew your voice or your calling and you dipped your toes into those waters and found the water much too cold. You probably saw the uphill battle it would be, to get from where you are to where you think God called you to be, so you chose another destination.

You're reading this book because you need to find your truth. God will challenge you, equip you, and anoint you to

God will challenge you, equip you, and anoint you to do His will.

do His will. In the beginning of time, Adam was given dominion over the earth. As descendants of Adam, that dominion has fallen to us. Everywhere we walk we are meant to make an impact for the glory of God.

You might be going through a difficult trial right now and you're wondering how in the world you're going to get out of this one. Your heart might be broken. You might have lost a child, a sibling, or parent. Your health might be deteriorating rapidly and the prognosis doesn't look good. People may have betrayed you whom you loved and trusted. You might be in a financial windfall and will soon be forced to ask others for help if something doesn't change quickly. Or maybe, like what happened to me, you've already hit rock bottom and don't know how things could possible get any worse.

Understand this – rock bottom experiences becomes the platform that allows you to help others. God knows your situation. He knows your struggle. He knows your failures and your worries. But the Lord

...rock bottom experiences becomes the platform that allows you to help others.

wants you to know that, in the valley is where many of His children find their voices. Your voice is your message.

Philippians 1:12 (NIV)

"Now I want you to know, brothers and sisters, that what has happened to me has actually served to advance the gospel."

Paul, who was once Saul, was in prison along with Timothy. He wrote this letter to the people of Philippi, Greece during his second missionary journey there. He found himself beaten and arrested for declaring the good news of salvation. Here's how this relates to you: what you're going through *really isn't about you*. I know it's hard to receive that, but it's the principles of the Kingdom.

You have to understand the ugly, vain, and pompous side of *"Christian Leaders,"* people who sit in their thrones of judgment and kick people out of their churches for man-made rules. They look down on people – demonstrating their overtly righteousness – forgetting the many sins they have been forgiven for. Pastors and leaders who have been in prison for committing crimes look down on those in the justice system. Women's leaders, who have had affairs or children out of wedlock, look down on pregnant teens. They have forgotten how to be relatable to this fallen world of broken people who are suffering. They have become gatekeepers to spiritual growth instead of gateways.

Whatever it is you are going through is for two reasons.

1.   To learn to trust in God and experience Him getting you out of your situation.

2.   To share what He has done in you and through you to others.

Paul wrote, "What has happened to me has actually served to advance the gospel!"

Remember, God will challenge you, equip you, and anoint you. What experiences have you been *challenged* with that have *equipped* you for God to *anoint* you to be a beacon of hope for others? I can't help anyone struck with the Bubonic Plague. Get this in your spirit – only those who have survived the Bubonic Plague can help others afflicted by it, via a blood transfusion. Their blood, their DNA, their voice, if you will, can help cure those affected by that deadly disease. Similarly, your past afflictions can now help others who are where you were.

Shake yourself from pity because of what you went through. Raise up your voice and tell others what God has done for you. Like the Psalmist wrote in the book of Psalm, Chapter 119, verse 71 (NIV):"It was good for me to be afflicted so that I might learn your decrees."

That which the enemy meant for evil, God will use for His glory. Whatever it is you may be going through now, don't be afraid. Yes, you will have trials and tribulations, but understand that they are meant to challenge, equip, and anoint you to walk out your mission.

I want to share with you a small piece of an upcoming letter I received from the Lord. The letter is entitled, **I have given you the tools, will you use them?**

At this time, I have assigned a task for My warriors who will be winning back the souls of My children. Will it be a hard task? Yes!

You may have been waiting for a sign from God - *when will I start using my gifts?* Here's the answer.... yesterday! You're already late. As soon as God did anything for you, as soon as he saved you – breathed life into you as he did Adam, and made you a new creature, you've been given a testimony to share with men and women.

The time is now. The question is, what will you do? What will you do with the talents you have been given?

What will you do with the talents you have been given?

Will you bury them in the sand or will you raise your voice and declare God's faithfulness from the mountaintops?

In an upcoming letter, entitled, **Your Choices Will Determine Your Outcome,** the Lord told me to write this:

My children, My Father has been patient. My children, My Father has been kind. My children, time is running out. These are the signs of the times. My return, My time is fast approaching.

Your message is built into your testimony. That's your voice. It's unique to you. It's part of your DNA and part the Father's DNA. I exhort you, challenge you, and encourage you to become an agent of change in your family, within your circle of influence, and your community. As God did with Moses and all those who were willing to carry the cross – you open your mouth and He will speak through you. Then, and only then, will you walk in your true power.

NOTES

What did God reveal to you in this chapter?

Chapter 6

Remove the Scales from Your Eyes

In the next phase of this book, you're going to read messages directly from the Divine Trinity: The Father, The Son, and the Holy Spirit. Among other things, these letters will reinforce to you that they are One.

Before you go on reading, I want you to open your heart, mind, and soul to receive Truth. The enemy of our souls has done a masterful job of making us wary and untrusting of one another. We can hear someone preach a message of life and salvation and we think he or she is only preaching for the money or fame. We see someone singing their heart out to the Lord and we think they are vain, conceited, and just putting on a show. In order to defeat the enemy, we need to know his tactics.

I pray that you remove the scales from your eyes. He that has an ear to hear, let him hear, he that has eyes to see, let him see. These letters you are about to read have been given to me miraculously.

Now, you have to understand, I have been a carrier and protector of man's law as a police officer for many years. Now, I'm a messenger of God's law. I have seen evil at a level that most people don't. I have also seen good Samaritans and great, selfless deeds done at a level that most don't. Out of my experiences, and mostly out of respect for my God, I don't use the word, *miraculously,* loosely.

But I don't know how else to explain that I am able to write a language thought long dead? A language that a Shaman from Egypt recognized. How else can I explain the fact that I can read it fluently and without effort, as if it were my first language? More so, how else can I explain that I can feel the writings, as if braille, and interpret them?

The best word I can use to describe it is a *miracle.* It should not be possible. But those of you who know the God I know, know the answer to this question: Is there anything too hard for God? He is the God of the impossible.

God desires to reveal his essence to you. Contained in these writings are love letters God cried out to me, just as He did in the days of old. There was always a warning and grace before destruction. God extended mercy and grace to Adam and Eve by not destroying them with they sinned in the Garden of Eden. God gave mercy and grace to mankind through Noah and his family. God gave mercy and grace to Lot, his wife, and their children when He destroyed Sodom and Gomorrah. God even gave mercy and grace to Jonah, who, when God told him to go to

Nineveh, intentionally and deliberately boarded a ship and sailed in the opposite direction.

I urge you not to be like Lot's life. God chose to save her amidst the thousands who died that day. Yet, because she was cynical, overly curious, and perhaps too much in love with the world, she defied God and looked back. Lot's wife, who had been spared, ended up killing herself by her disobedience. As you read these letters, don't look back. Look forward. Press onward to what God has in store for you.

Not all the letters are *love letters.* A good father never shies away from correcting, admonishing, and even rebuking his children. Good children, people who are planted in good soil, soak up the corrections and alter their courses. We recognize our sinful ways to strive to receive the prize of salvation that is offered free to all mankind.

I remember when I went on a sabbatical. I wanted to complain to the Lord about the people around me. The Lord began to show me, *me.* The Lord said, "You like to argue," He then began to show me every argument I had ever been in. He said, "When you argue, it pierces my spirit. I choose you and, because you are my child, it grieves my soul when you argue." The last thing I ever want to do is grieve my Father's soul. It doesn't matter to me what man thinks of me. However, it matters what God thinks of me.

One thing I know in my heart is this – God is ready to use you. *Now.* God wants you to experience a more abundant life. He wants you to know the inner peace that comes from trusting in Him. He wants you to know the feeling of satisfaction and joy one gets when they walk out their calling. But you have to understand, time is running out. No one has an infinite amount of time here on earth. No one. God is looking for people who understand – as it is in heaven so shall it be on earth, for the Kingdom of God is at hand.

True Power

I declare over you in the name of Jesus, you are about to step into a season of GREAT Explosion. The gifts that have been lying dormant inside of you are going to start percolating. They are going to compel you into action.

You may have heard it said, *Knowledge is Power.* As I think of that statement, I don't believe it anymore. If you don't use the knowledge, how does it serve you? It's like having faith, if you don't exercise your faith, how does it serve you? The Bible says, faith, without works (or action), is dead. In the same way, knowledge is powerless unless it is utilized.

It's not enough for you to believe that God is about to launch you into working for His Kingdom. It's not enough for you to believe you have been called by God to do something. It's not enough for you to believe that God has given you a message or talents that will enhance His Kingdom on earth. None of that really matters. What matters is that you act on it.

The Time is Now; Awaken Your Dormant Gifts

Open up your heart, let the world's perspective fall away...
turn the page and read the words of the Father.

See Him as He sees you, through the eyes of unsurpassed,
unceasing, and unyielding love.

NOTES

What did God reveal to you in this chapter?

Letters From God

1 - I AM THAT I AM

My children,

I send you greetings from our Lord and Savior Jesus Christ. The time has come to unveil truth. Truth of the I AM, THAT I AM, the Creator of all.

Many have tried to distort who I AM for their own gain, but who I AM is about you. You are my children. My creation.

I formed you in the image of Myself for you to know the love that I share for all. As time has passed, who I AM and what I have desired for you has been washed and removed.

I AM here to tell you I love you beyond anything you can imagine.

You are my precious creation.

There is so much I desire for each of you. What you have become is the view you have taken on from man and not that of the Father. Each of you hold a key to all that I have given. Due to the division, you have forgotten the Oneness of who you are.

What I desire for you is unity for the sake of all. You have the power that dwells within. The power and dominion was given to you from the foundation. Though the foundation is unsettled it is not unable to stand, for on this rock I shall build my church.

You my people are the church. Christ is the solid foundation.

In due season, I will make Myself - The I AM THAT I AM true and real to you as the God of your forefathers, The God of Abraham, The God of Isaac, and The God of Jacob (Israel).

2 - CRY FROM GOD

My child,

I bring you greetings from Our Lord and Savior, Jesus Christ. Things in life may be difficult to understand, but I walk with you, I talk with you, and I will never forsake you.

When darkness of life arises, I bring you into the light. I shine upon you. Remember who wakes you up in the morning and who lays you down at night. You are My precious child.

When you have needs in life, I will supply them to you. When you have heartaches, I will heal them. Remember always to seek Me first in all things, and they shall be given unto you. The doors of heaven pour out abundant blessings to all My children who are willing to receive them.

I have not forgotten My children. My children, have you forgotten Me? When I have called on them to do My Will, they closed the doors. Yet when they call on Me, My doors are always open.

Remember when I entered your life? I will be there. When people around you can't see My beauty, share the beauty of God with them.

My children are lost. They are calling and crying out for My love. My love is warm. My love is sweet. My love is there for all who need it.

Show the love I have for each of you to everyone around you. When they see the love I have in you, they will feel the love I have for all.

Peace! Peace! Let My children feel, see, and believe in peace. My children are in turmoil. They need peace.

Show peace in your lives; experience peace in your lives. Share the peace.

My love is here for all. I never left any of My children, despite what many may say.

My children have all been given the ability of choice. They choose to leave Me and forsake Me. The weight of the world and the state of the world needs to be evaluated by all.

I am here. Seek Me out in all things. I am here.

Spread the words I have shared with you. I am here. I will always be here. Call on Me and I will answer.

Peace be unto you, My children.

Peace be unto you.

I love you all, and I am the I Am and the God of all.

Peace.

3 – The Coma of Life

My children,

I send you greetings from Our Lord and Savior, Jesus Christ. Our Father is crying many, many tears over the selfishness His children have for Him.

My children, without regard for Our Father, Who sits up high and looks down low, we go from day to day not recognizing that it is Our Father Who sustains us from day to day, hour to hour.

You could have been sleeping in your graves, but Our Father chose to wake you up that you may serve Him and do His Will. That is all He has asked of us. Yet those of you who are in your right minds, able to speak, able to walk, and able to do God's Will, continue to live for right now.

My children, living in the right now is not going to get you into the Gates of Glory.

My children, I need warriors who will win back the souls of My children. I desire and need a church without spot or wrinkle. The church I seek is a godly church. One that is not afraid to speak My Name, and one that will fight My battles against the demons that are set out to destroy all I am putting together.

Some of you, My children, see the evils of the world that are manifesting in our children, in men and women. Children are killing their parents. Parents are killing their children. Husbands are killing their wives. Wives are killing their husbands, and neighbors are killing their neighbors – not only in the flesh, but also in the spiritual sense.

My children are being possessed by demons and some are blind; they cannot see the writing on the wall.

My children, you need to wake up!

I sent a Comforter to be with you and that is the Holy Spirit. Know who you are in Christ for My Name's sake.

If you do not know me, seek Me. I will never leave you nor will I forsake you. I will be there for you and with you until the very end.

The end is fast approaching; therefore, you must get your house in order. No one knows the hour or the second of My return, but I will come as a thief in the night.

Get your house in order. Tell everyone you can, "Get your house in order." But before you do, make sure your spiritual house is in order.

My children, read My Words and live My Word: Matthew 10, Isaiah 20, Ezekiel 3, Matthew 7, Ephesians 2, and Revelation 20. My children, when I give you a Word to read, study it, speak My Words out loud, and live My Words. They were given for your instruction to everyday living, praying, meditating, and feeling the holy anointed power of our Almighty Father.

My children, don't waste valuable time living in the fast world of sin. Satan has tried to persuade you away from Me, the Almighty Loving God.

My children, I love you. I have given you the key to everlasting life. Salvation is free. Despite what people have said, I sent My Son down that you might be saved and set free of your sins. Go and sin no more, My children. Walk in the newness of life in which you were called to walk.

Don't be afraid to speak My Name. Feel the power when you say My Name, Jesus. When times get hard, say it over and over, Jesus, Jesus, and watch the anointing fall upon you. Speak My Name in your darkest hour and watch the light of My Will transform.

Don't be ashamed, My children. Don't be ashamed. I will be returning for a church without spot or wrinkle. I've gone to prepare a place for you. If it were not so, I would have told you.

Look to the hills from which cometh thy help.

My children, I love you all; but even as I give you these letters, I know still some of you will not receive them. But for those of you that do and do My will, I will see you in glory.

My children, despite what many have said, I am real. I am with you. I have never forsaken you, even when you have turned your backs on Me.

I will continue to comfort and keep you. My children, I love you and My Father loves you.

In Jesus' name, go and peace be with you.

4 - I HAVE GIVEN YOU THE TOOLS. WILL YOU USE THEM?

My children,

My Heart is aching. My Heart is bleeding, and My Heart is wounded. No one sees the pain I feel for My children.

I have directed My children. I have given My children the tools, but yet, they still choose to close the door to everlasting life.

At this time, I have assigned a task for My warriors who will be winning back the souls of My children. Will it be a hard task? "Yes!" My children have been misled by Satan. He has given them things of the world that appear to be irresistible.

Irresistible to the point My children have lost sight of what I too have promised them. I've promised My children houses and land, a stream that flows of milk and honey, streets that are paved with gold, and EVERLASTING LIFE.

Yet My children seek to have fast money, fast cars, and items that were not given from Me. Why is this? They are impatient. They want things right now. But all of those things I did not give to them and all the things that were given to them by Satan. Satan stole it right from under them. Quick money goes as quickly as it comes.

I have told My children, I have promised My children, if they would only wait upon the Lord, if they would only be obedient in My Name, all things shall be given unto them.

My children, hear Me and hear Me well. Living in the right now will not get you into heaven. You must look to the hills from which cometh thy help.

Trust and believe God will do all He said He would do. You must trust Our Father Who sits up high. My children, I love you all. I have given you the tools to eternal salvation, but yet you continue to turn your backs.

What will it take? If I were to turn My back on you, this world would come to a sure end. The devil would take full control, and all would fall into eternal damnation.

I will not turn My back on you. I will continue to be Your Father, the One Who will comfort you, the One Who will love you until the very end, and the One Who will guide you in the time of storm, the One and Only, the True I Am.

My children, hear My plea, hear My cry, and listen to My Words. Time is running out. Precious time is fast approaching to an end.

What stand will you take? Will you stand up and be counted as a warrior of Christ for Our Father, Lord God? The key to eternal life begins now! Ask Me to enter into your life. Re-dedicate yourselves to My Father. Let Us see that We will not be alone.

I have prepared a place for you. Will you come in? The tools have been placed right before you. Will you use them, or will you allow them to sit?

My children, the time has come for you to make a decision. Read My Words: Revelation 3, Revelation 5, Revelation 12, and Revelation 19. If you do not believe that My return is fast approaching, read My Words. Live My Words.

Feel My presence and expect My return. My children, I am calling My brides home. Will your name be on the roll to eternal life? I want you there. Do you want to be there?

I have given you the tools. Use them.

Until then, My children... until then.

5 - WARRIORS FOR CHRIST

My children,

I send you greetings from Our Lord and Savior, Jesus Christ, Who sits up high and looks down low, the Protector of all, the One Who guides and leads you in the path of righteousness for His Name's sake.

My good and faithful servants, the time is drawing nigh. I need for you to be obedient in My Name. Study My Word. Eat of it until you are full. Fill yourselves and allow My Word to fill you until your cup overflows with abundant blessings.

My children, in the end time, My Word is the only thing you will have to stand on. Faith, understanding, truth, love, and the all-knowing knowledge of your Father, Who will be with you and never forsake you.

My children, the trumpets are sounding. Time, precious time, is running out. The time has come for you to get your house in order.

When I say your house, I am referring to your spiritual house — your soul, your spirit, the inner man. If you have not accepted Me as your Savior, ask Me to come into you so you might be saved, that someday you may see Me in glory. My Father and I are waiting. Ask of it and it shall be given unto you. Change is something that can happen in a split second.

If you trust and believe on Me and in Me, it will happen. Trust Me. Believe in Me. I am the Comforter. I am all that you will need if you will allow Me to enter.

I have cried many, many tears because of the earthly pain I see My children going through. Some of them can't see the light because their minds, their spirits are so cloudy; but if they only knew I can remove all of the clouds in their lives.

Some of them are so drunk they cannot see past their hands. If they only knew, if they would only ask Me to take the taste from their mouth, I will deliver them.

Some of them are filled with drugs. They can't even stand to know that if they would only, I would lift them to their feet, if they only believed in Me.

Some of them are so deaf. They can't hear the Holy Spirit when it is trying to minister to them, to direct them in the right path.

Many of My children will die, not knowing Me as their Savior. Don't let it be you. Don't let time run out on you before you accept Me into your life. I'm calling My brides to glory. Will you be there to have your named called from My roll?

I need warriors who will fight My fight. Through it all, I need children who will stand up for My Name and not be ashamed.

Time is running out. The trumpets are sounding. Get ready. Get ready.

Ready My Words: Ephesians 4, I Corinthians 2, Genesis 12:1, Matthew 4, I Thessalonians 3. I need children who are not afraid to stand on My Name and on My Word.

Speak My Words out loud and watch the miracles that will start to transform your lives. Live My Word and watch how your lives will change. Pass My Words along and watch how other lives will be touched, just by passing My Words along.

Fear should not be in your vocabulary. Fear is of the devil and allows you not to receive your blessings.

I will not forsake you, but I will keep you in My loving arms, shielding you from thy enemies. Will you have tests and trials? Yes, they will make you strong. I need strong warriors.

The time has come for My warriors to start training, so they may assist Me in winning over more warriors.

You see, My children, no one knows the hour when I shall return. My children, in time I will be returning. Get your house in order! Tell your family. Tell your friends. Tell people you don't know they need to get their house in order. But, before you do, make sure your house is in order. Work on yourselves first.

Read and live My Word. Eat it like it's your last meal. For without it, no nourishment shall be obtained.

Don't be afraid of the gifts I will be showering down on each of you. I will use some to be evangelists, some preachers, some teachers, some prophets; some will be given the gift of healing words and hands.

Whatever I give you, continue to raise your hands to the heavens from which your blessings came.

If you are unsure of the gifts I have given you, pray for understanding, and wisdom shall be given unto you. For whatever gift is given unto you, know it has been given from Our Father Who sits on high. Give Him continued praise.

Praise Him! Praise Him and watch His Work unfold.

Will you take a stand for Christ? Will you take a stand for Our Lord Father God? Don't get discouraged. Don't fret. Don't worry. Don't think your work will go in vain.

Many will hear you, but only a few will listen and receive God. For those that do, they will see Our Father in heaven Who is waiting for His good and faithful servants.

Peace be unto you until we shall meet again in glory.

6 - FALSE PROPHETS

My children,

I send you greetings from Our Lord and Savior, Jesus Christ. My children are in great turmoil. Without due regard, they have allowed man, their leaders, to destroy everything that I have put together.

Because My children are in great turmoil, I hear them crying from the wilderness because they are lost.

My children are in great pain mentally, physically, and spiritually. Their leaders have led them astray.

My children have listened to these false prophets who say they have come in the Name of the Lord and given My children false doctrines.

As a result, many, many religions have come forth as a result of the false teachings.

I will be coming back for My Church. My Church will be My people who believe on Me and in Me. My Church will be without spot or wrinkle. My Church will cross all barriers of race and religions.

The time has come for My children to speak truth and only truth. There will continue to be false prophets who say they come in the Name of the Lord; but pray and I will give you the ability to see which is trash and which is good.

My children, false prophets are cunning wolves in sheep's clothing. They will try to win you over, but you must pray to Our Father God in heaven and ask Him to give you the ability to discern.

My children, the evils of the world are trying to destroy all that I am putting together for the good of My people. Everyone who cries out saying, "Lord! Lord!" will not enter into the Kingdom of heaven.

They will say, "Didn't I do Your will? Didn't I cast out demons?" But I will say to them, "Get away from Me, you evil people, because you did not do My Will, but the will of the devil."

You see, My children, just as I have given gifts to My children, the devil, Satan, has done the same; but you will know the fruit of My children because it will be good. The fruit of Satan shall and will be bad. A good tree cannot bear bad fruit and a bad tree cannot bear good fruit.

My children, stop living in the right now and start living in My Name. It's not hard, not if you look to the hills from which cometh thy help.

I will never forsake you nor will I ever lead you astray. I will never turn My back on you nor will I leave your side. When times get hard, when things seem a little rough, when you are at your darkest hour, I will be there to carry you through your storm.

My children, I love you and My Father loves you. Let Us see that We will not be alone in glory. My Father has prepared houses and land, a stream that flows of milk and honey, and streets that are paved with gold. The doors are open to anyone who is willing to do My Will.

My children, you shall be rewarded for your job well done.

Go in peace, My children. Your work begins now. Spread My Words, read My Words, live My Words, and speak My Words.

Love your Father, Almighty God.

7 - YOUR CHOICES OF TODAY WILL DETERMINE YOUR OUTCOME

My children,

Greetings in the Name of Our Father in heaven Who sits up high and looks down low. My children, the choices you have made today were set forth from the beginning of time.

From the very beginning, I designed you that you would live an everlasting life in the Garden of Eden. The first man was enticed by the first woman to eat from the tree of knowledge, which was forbidden. And from that time, My children, choices were given: either to adhere to the Word of God or to do as you please.

My children, Satan tries to entice you to do what is wrong; however, you have the ability to do what is right. The devil cannot force you to do what is wrong. You have free will.

My children, in giving you free will, some of you carry on in life as if there are no consequences to your actions. As a child, you are to be disciplined by your Father.

My children, if you do not turn from your wicked ways, My children, you will suffer the wrath of God.

My children, My Father in heaven has given you chance after chance, but you continue to disobey Him.

Just as in the days of Sodom and Gomorrah, where sin ran rampant, it was accepted as if it were okay. Those who sinned were destroyed.

This world will come to a quick end. Those who do not turn from their wicked ways will be destroyed if they do not acknowledge Me, your Savior, and ask for forgiveness and sin no more.

My children, do not continue to be disobedient! Do not allow the sins of the world to overcome you. You need to overcome the sins of today. God will give you the strength to do it, if you believe.

In the end, My Father in heaven shall reign in the Promised Land. My Father is the Lord of lords and King of kings.

Satan is out to seek and destroy what God is building up for His people. If you continue to sin, and you do not run from your wicked ways, you will find a fiery pit called hell, where you will suffer for eternity.

My children, My Father has been patient. My children, My Father has been kind. My children, time is running out. These are the signs of the times. My return, My time, is fast approaching.

You choose, My children, to accept My warning or discount it as being false. My children, no man, no woman, no child knows the hour, the second, nor the day of My return.

You need to get your house in order, My children. Stop playing church. Stop pretending and putting on a front for your fellow man. God knows your heart.

Walk in the calling in which you have been designed for. If you ask for forgiveness and sin no more, My children, in heaven shall you see your reward.

During your walk, Satan will try to destroy what God is trying to build for His people. You can resist the devil. Our Father in Heaven will protect you, My children, if you believe it, you shall receive it.

If you allow yourself to be weakened by the temptations of life, you will not be able to fight the battle for God, Our Father in Heaven.

Our Father is seeking a strong body of people who will put their faith totally in Him.

My children, these are the last and evil days. You need to get prepared. My children, My Father has had you in training for millions of years. The time has come for Our Father's good soldiers to put on their armor and prepare for battle.

The devil knows your weaknesses and he will throw them at you to see if you will buckle.

My children, study My Word. It has been written in the Book of Revelation as to what is expected to come in the end time.

Some of you do not believe in the Book of Revelation. It has been written that one will come who will try to represent himself as the Living Christ.

Many of you will be deceived because you did not prepare yourselves.

My children, if there is something you do not understand about the last and evil days, pray and ask Our Father in Heaven for understanding.

The devil, Satan, is building up a people, false prophets, who will try to draw you in. You will be able to distinguish them from the fruit they bear.

If they be of God, they will bear good fruit. Not everyone will accept My child, Edith Darling, but she is a True Prophet of God. Her ministry will bear good fruit, for she has been given many gifts and she shall go to the nations to spread My Word.

You can choose, My children, to receive it or reject it. It is up to you. Do not miss out, My children. Do not be deceived!

My children, time is running out. My time, My return, is fast approaching.

I am raising up a people who will not be afraid to speak My Word. I am raising up a people who will fight a good battle.

My children, the task I have set for you will not be easy. I need a bold people who will stand up for Christ. In the process, the unbelievers will try to attack you from every angle.

Even some of those I have placed in authority over you will doubt, but My Word will be manifested.

My children, when you turn from your evil ways and dedicate your life for the task I have set ahead for you, in heaven shall you reap your rewards.

I need radicals for Christ. I will fill My children with the Holy Anointed Spirit and give them the gifts as I did on the Day of Pentecost.

I am raising up My children from all walks of life, from all corners of the world. Not one child is more special than the other. They are all out for the same purpose. They are out to win over more soldiers for My Father.

My Father needs, My Father deserves, My children, My Father desires a strong army of people who without question will pick up the cross and follow Me.

My children, the battle will not be easy. The road will be hard to trod. If you pick up My cross and follow Me, My children, in heaven shall you reap your reward.

My Father and I have prepared a place for you in heaven, My Child.

When the load gets hard to carry, look to the hills from which cometh thy help.

When your friends, when your family, and the people you do not know talk about you, tell them you are a child of God. Your walk with Christ will be proof enough of who you say you are.

When people call you crazy and look at you in disbelief, tell them you are crazy for God and continue in your walk with Him.

During this time, you will not be alone, My children. I will be there to carry you through your toughest times. I will be there to dry your tears. I will be there to pick you up when you have fallen. I will be there to make you strong when you become weak.

My children, continue to keep the faith. Believe in Me, Your Father and Lord Savior, Jesus Christ. I will not let you down. Believe in Me.

Be strong in faith and be encouraged, My faithful servants.

These words I send you are from Our Lord and Savior, Jesus Christ. Peace be with you until We meet again.

8 - THE LAST AND EVIL DAYS

My children,

Evil is in the air. Take heed, My children. If you do not believe we are living in the last and evil days, read My Words of the Lord Father Who sits up high and looks down low. Read My Words and ponder no more: Ecclesiastes 3, Romans 6, Revelation 12, Hebrews 12.

The time has come for My children to take a stand. It is time to stop playing and start performing. Evil has tried to take full control of My people. However, My children have been blinded by evil and think it is I.

I, as well as the devil, can duplicate blessings. He wants to tempt you with the things of this world and come in the Name of Jesus and then come right back and steal your joy, your happiness, your very beings away.

Why is this, My children? Because you do not have the mind enough to say, "This did not come from God." You did not seek Me when you received it to verify that, in fact, it came from Me.

Yes, you thanked Me, but you did not seek Me. I shook My head in disbelief and dismay.

If you cannot seek Me first in "All things! All things!" you will be lost forever.

You will not have the ability to survive the tests and trials you and all God's children will be facing in these last and evil days.

My children, My children, the trumpets are sounding! I am calling My brides home. You need to have the power of the Holy Ghost to sustain you through these times.

There is no joke here, My children. These are perilous times and you need to get ready, get ready! You need the armor of God's protection around you all the time. As you like to say, "24/7."

My children, I give you these warnings not to scare you, but to forewarn you of what is to be.

I will be returning for a church without spot or wrinkle. The time has come for you to clean up your act now. The devil will be coming at you with full force and you need to have the ability to discern if it is Me, God Almighty – or the devil, the deceitful.

Many people will begin to say they have come in the Name of Jesus, but they have not. They will even put on a great show for you, but they have not come from Me. They have come to deceive you and you are going to be.

You will need to be prepared for what the devil has in store for you.

My children, I love you and My Father loves you. We have cried many, many tears for you, but you continue to turn your backs on Me.

Yes, I too have showered down blessings time after time, but you did not recognize Me; and now that the devil is giving you blessings, you now try to reverence Me.

You need the power of the Holy Spirit to discern the difference. If you have not awakened the Holy Spirit that is your source of communication to Me, you need to do it and do it now.

It is time to stop playing, My children, and start performing in My Namesake. I have given each of you gifts, some I have stored in you many gifts. Utilize your gifts and use them in the Name of Jesus.

"Do not use your gifts for self-gain. Use them only as I direct you to."

My children, My children, time is drawing nigh. Time is fast approaching of My return. It is time to prepare yourselves and get under the umbrella of God. If you do not, you will be lost forever in sin.

You recognize the time you are living in, but you say over and over, "I have time!" Live these days as if they were your last, because you are not promised tomorrow, My children.

You are not promised tomorrow, My children. I breathe life into you and I know the day and time of your departure from this land.

Read My Words: Ephesians 6. My children, the trumpets are sounding. Get ready, get ready.

My children, I leave you with these words. My Father and I have prepared many mansions for you, streams that flow of milk and honey, streets that are paved with gold. If it were not so, I would have told you.

My children, the time has come for you to make a choice, to walk with Me and not turn from Me anymore.

Time is running out, My children. As time goes on, I will direct your paths. Wait and listen. Do not jump at the sound of My voice. Be patient and move in My Name, for there is much work that needs to be done.

As for forgiveness, repent daily of your sins in My Name. Rededicate yourselves to Me. Walk in the newness in which you have been called to walk. Go, My children, and sin no more. Become all you can be and have been designed to be in My Name.

My children, stop walking in today and walk in the position in which you were ordained to walk.

So many of My children will die not knowing Me; not because they were not told, but because they chose not to receive Me.

Time is running out. Get your house in order, My children. Get your spiritual house in order.

My Father and I are waiting. Go and walk in the newness. Peace be unto you. Until We meet again.

9 – My Love is

My children,

My heart is aching; it is slowly tearing apart. For I speak to you, I give to you, but you are not hearing Me.

The love I share for you is greater than any other love you will ever know on this earth. No man, woman, or child can give you the love My Father and I share for you.

My child, hear Me and hear Me well.

"I will not forsake you. I will not give up on you. I will not turn My back on you. I will be there to encourage you, to lift you up when you are down. When others turn their backs on you, I will be there to comfort you."

This is the kind of love I share for you, My children. When you are hungry, I will feed you. When you are without clothes, I will clothe you. When you need shelter, I will give you shelter.

Love is about trust. If you would only trust Me, I will supply your needs and give you the desires of your heart.

My children, in the end time, you will need to be able to distinguish Me from Satan. Satan is out to seek and destroy. Satan is also out to emulate Me in the end time. Do not be deceived. Do not be blind. Pray your eyes will be opened and not closed to deception.

My child, My Father Who sits up high and looks down low, sends you this message and warning in the Name of Our Lord and Savior Jesus Christ because He needs for His Church, His children, His brides to be prepared for what the devil is trying to seek and destroy.

My children, through the love I share for you, you need to be strong. Do not become weak-minded; stay in the Word. For in the end time, the promises of God and the Word of God is all you will have to stand on.

I am raising up a people who will not be ashamed, nor afraid to speak My Word.

Will you be able to stand up and take on the feat I have prepared for you?

Not everyone will be able to pick up the cross and follow Me and fight the battle that is out to seek and destroy what My Father in heaven is building for His people.

My Father needs, My Father desires, My Father deserves a strong army of people who are not afraid to take a stand for Christ.

I pray you will not be left behind. I pray I will see you in heaven. It will be a grand day. Do not miss out, My children, for the reward will be great in heaven.

For when this earth has passed away, in heaven will you find your reward. My Father and I have prepared a place for you. I want you to reap the rewards. Do not miss out. The trumpets are sounding, get ready, get ready! Do not miss out.

My children, My Father and I are waiting on you. Take up My cross and follow Me. The road will not be easy. The road will be hard to trod. There will be a heavy load to carry. If you are willing to take up My cross and follow Me, I will protect you every step of the way.

Your family and friends may not want to go. Your husband, your wife, your children, may not want to go. If you take up this cross, sometimes you have to go alone.

Leave them behind. The works they see in you, the boldness they see in you, will draw them in. Allow the love of God, My Father, to shine in you that wherever you go, it will be indisputable you are a child of God.

My children, remember that I love you and I will never forsake you. I am the Alpha, the Omega, the Beginning and the End, El-Shaddai, and Jehovah. I am the Potter and you are My clay.

I will mold you into the man and woman I have designed you to be. Trust Me, love Me, depend solely on Me. I will take you through the storm, through the rain, and through the fire.

These words I send you, My children, are from Our Father and Lord Savior, Jesus Christ.

Until we meet again, Peace be unto you.

Chapter 7

Now What?

It's time to see yourself as God sees you. He doesn't see you as your nationality, ethnicity, sex, age, or income status. He doesn't see you as flawed, unworthy, guilt-ridden, broken, or by the labels others see you – or even by the way the father of lies allows you to see yourself so that you don't think you're going to do great things in your life.

The God of our forefathers, yes, *that* God, sees you covered by the precious blood of the Lamb. Your sins of the past have been washed and you have been made whole because He sent His Son, Jesus, to die for the sins of all mankind. He now sees you as His beautiful bride. A bride without a spot, blemish, or wrinkle.

People saw Moses as a stutterer, God saw him as a liberator. Jessie didn't even consider young David as someone worthy to meet the prophet, let alone to be in line to become the next king, God saw David as a giant killer.

I declare you free from whatever guilt-trip the devil has played on your mind and emotions. In God's hands, you are powerful. Jesus left a proclamation when he said, "Verily, verily I say unto you, He that believeth in me, the works that I do shall he do also; and greater works than these shall he do..." John 14:12

I pray that, as you've read this book, God has revealed his Truth and the scales of this world have been removed from your eyes. Take the messages learned in this book and apply them to your life. Harness the power of God in your life and manifest the calling He has had for you since the beginning of time.

Take the messages learned in this book and apply them to your life.

You have been assigned a territory. That territory is different for everyone. It could be in your own backyard, beginning with your family and extended family members. It could be your church or in your job. It could be women who are hurting. It could be men who need to learn how to become true men of God in their homes. It could be that you are called to affect policy and law. Whatever your territory is, take dominion of it. Walk in the authority given to you by the Father.

One thing I know is, when you bring our Father into your territory with you, in the spiritual world, the ground will shake wherever your feet tread.

The God of our forefather, The God of Abraham, The God of Isaac, and The God of Jacob (Israel), *that* God, The I AM That I AM, has called you to awaken people to His truth. Stand tall and proclaim what He has done for you, in you, and through you.

Get off the sidelines. You are called for a greater purpose. God has prepared you for a great battle.

This Modern Day Revelation, The Time is Now; Awaken Your Dormant Gifts, is for God's people around the world.

Now that your dormant gifts have been awakened, awaken truth in your communities. Buy copies of this book to share with your neighbors, friends, co-workers and those you meet on the street.

If you would like to invite me to speak to your church, college or group, please, contact me at AwakenYourDormantGifts@gmail.com

Peace and Blessings –

Edie Darling

NOTES

What did God reveal to you in this chapter?

About the Author

Edie Darling is a Dynamic Motivational Speaker, A Visionary, and a true Humanitarian. She is a law enforcement veteran and a minister of the Gospel since 1998. Edie has formerly served as the Senior Chaplain in the Department of Detention and Corrections as the Supervisor of Religious Services.

Edie is the founder of: *End Time Message Ministries, Wake Up With Edie Darling*, and *3 Is Enough*. Her vision is to build bridges of compassion by reintroducing Nations back to the One True Living God; The God of Abraham, The God of Isaac, and The God of Jacob (Israel).

As a respected and sought after religious leader, her message transcends across all religions and, as a result, she is able to connect people of all faiths as she carries a modern-day revelation of ancient prophetic messages of Faith, Hope, and Love to the Nations. Her message motivates and encourages everyone to look beyond themselves and to humanity as a whole.

For speaking opportunities, please email: AwakenYourDormantGifts.com

Acknowledgments

I would like to thank my mother Susie Siplin, my father, the late Tommy Lee Siplin, and the late aunt Dora Thomas, who always encouraged me to do what is right, never lose sight of a dream, but most importantly to remember who I am, a Siplin by birth. There is strength and integrity in that name. As my daddy would say, "Riches and fame I cannot give you. All I have is my name. Don't bring shame to my name." Here's to you, Daddy.

I would like to thank my husband, Christopher Guay, for keeping me on my toes and for being one of my biggest cheerleaders - without the pom poms of course. Thank you for your unyielding love and support.

To our children, Jeremy, Candice, Alexis, and Aaron who continuously challenge us to stay before the throne daily.

To my spiritual mother, Bishop Vanessa Smith. Thank you for allowing me to be who I am in God and for supporting me spiritually on this journey.

To my mentor, Pastor Naomi Powell. Thank you for taking me under your wing and helping me to soar free like an eagle.

To my godly counsel, Shannon Erickson, thank you for pointing me back to the beginning and for reminding me... it's okay to be me.

To Ms. Marieta Harper of the Library of Congress. Thank you for being the one *yes* in the midst of a thousand *nos*. Thank you for your boldness, commitment, and dedication to finding and revealing truth.

Thank you, Eli Gonzalez, for drawing out of me that which God has poured in so that others might see through His lens.

To my big sister, Shara Stubbins, thank you for always having my back and for believing in me.

To my doctor, Dr. John Paul Gonzalvo. Thank you for being what I call a "Cold Case File Detective." God allowed you to see through His eyes and be His hands to do what some said was impossible. God used you to not only diagnose my rare condition but He also used you to save my life for such a time as this.

And to all of my friends who have stood the test of time with me... Get Ready, Get Ready, Get Ready!

NOTES

Edie Darling

The Time Is Now; Awaken Your Dormant Gifts

Edie Darling